I am a living thing

Bobbie Kalman

Crabtree Publishing Company

www.crabtreebooks.com

Created by Bobbie Kalman

For our beautiful little Alina
We welcome you to the world.

**Author and
Editor-in-Chief**
Bobbie Kalman

Editors
Reagan Miller
Robin Johnson

Photo research
Crystal Sikkens

Design
Bobbie Kalman
Katherine Berti
Samantha Crabtree (cover)

Production coordinator
Katherine Berti

Illustrations
Barbara Bedell: pages 6, 24

Photographs
© Dreamstime.com: pages 8 (top left), 15 (fruit), 19 (world), 24 (skeleton)
© iStockphoto.com: front cover, pages 3 (except butterfly), 8 (bottom right),
    9 (top left), 11 (top), 12, 16 (girl), 24 (eye and girl with water)
© 2008 Jupiterimages Corporation: page 5 (top)
© ShutterStock.com: back cover, pages 1, 3 (butterfly), 4, 5 (bottom), 6, 7,
    8 (bottom left), 9 (all except top left), 10, 11 (bottom and inset), 13, 14,
    15 (leaves and boy), 17 (girl), 18, 19 (all except world), 20, 21, 22, 23,
    24 (chick, middle three girls, plant)
Other images by Adobe Image Library, Comstock, and Photodisc

Library and Archives Canada Cataloguing in Publication

Kalman, Bobbie, 1947-
    I am a living thing / Bobbie Kalman.

(Introducing living things)
Includes index.
ISBN 978-0-7787-3229-7 (bound).--ISBN 978-0-7787-3253-2 (pbk.)

    1. Human biology--Juvenile literature. I. Title. II. Series.

QP37.K335 2007   j612   C2007-904898-6

The Library of Congress has cataloged the printed edition as follows:
Kalman, Bobbie.
    I am a living thing / Bobbie Kalman.
        p. cm. -- (Introducing living things)
    Includes index.
    ISBN-13: 978-0-7787-3229-7 (rlb)
    ISBN-10: 0-7787-3229-0 (rlb)
    ISBN-13: 978-0-7787-3253-2 (pb)
    ISBN-10: 0-7787-3253-3 (pb)
    1. Human biology--Juvenile literature. 2. Biology--Juvenile literature.
I. Title. II. Series.

QP37.K35 2008
612--dc22
                                                    2007031487

Crabtree Publishing Company

Printed in Canada/012013/DM20121114

www.crabtreebooks.com   1-800-387-7650

Published in Canada
Crabtree Publishing
616 Welland Ave.
St. Catharines, Ontario
L2M 5V6

Published in the United States
Crabtree Publishing
PMB 59051
350 Fifth Avenue, 59th Floor
New York, New York 10118

Published in the United Kingdom
Crabtree Publishing
Maritime House
Basin Road North, Hove
BN41 1WR

Published in Australia
Crabtree Publishing
3 Charles Street
Coburg North
VIC, 3058

Contents

Am I a living thing?   4

I am made of cells   6

I am all that!   8

What do I need?   10

I need water   11

I need air   12

I need sunlight   13

I need energy   14

I need food!   16

I need people   18

I need other things   20

I grow and change   22

Words to know and Index   24

Am I a living thing?

Am I a living thing? Plants are living things. Animals are living things. People are living things, too. I am a person. I am a living thing.

Living things need air, water, and food. Most living things also need sunshine. I need air, water, food, and sunshine. I need plants and animals. I need a place to live. I need people who love me.

I am made of cells

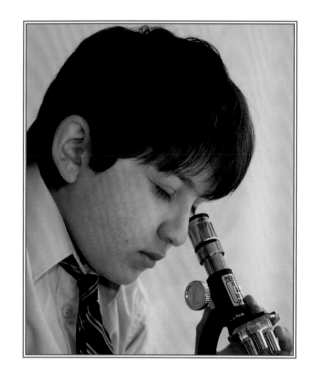

I am made up of tiny things called **cells**. You can see cells only with a **microscope**. Some living things have just one cell. Other living things have many kinds of cells. People have many kinds of cells. The cells shown here are all in our bodies.

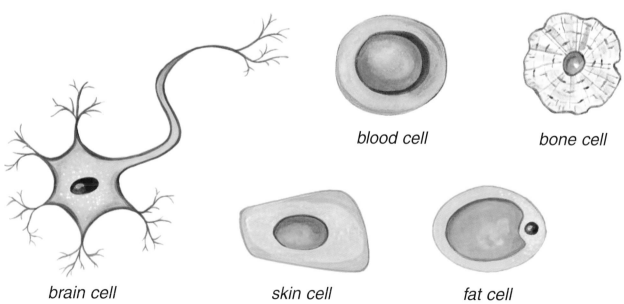

blood cell

bone cell

brain cell

skin cell

fat cell

Blood flows through our bodies. Which cells are blood cells? **Nerve cells** tell us when we are cold or hurt. Which are nerve cells? **Brain cells** make our bodies work. Skin cells cover our bodies.

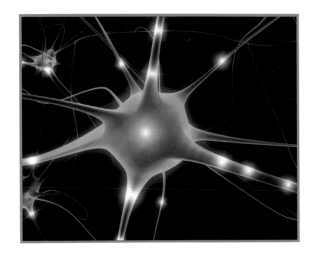

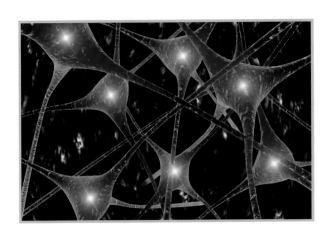

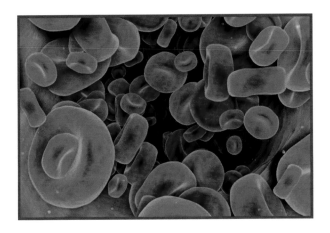

Answers:

The blue cells are nerve cells. The beige cells above are skin cells. The orange cells are brain cells. The red cells are blood cells. Which ones did you get right?

I am all that!

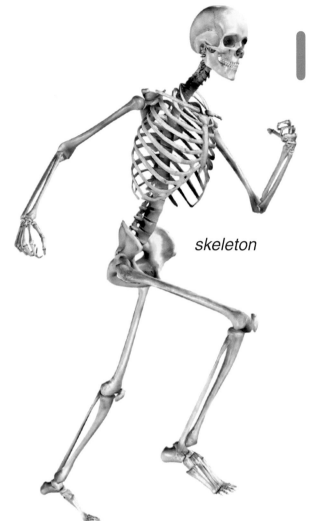

skeleton

I am a **mammal**. Mammals are animals with hair or fur on their bodies. Mammals have **backbones** and **skeletons** inside their bodies. Living things with backbones and skeletons are called **vertebrates**. I have a backbone and a skeleton. I am a vertebrate.

Big brains

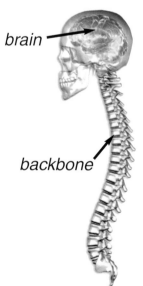

brain

backbone

Vertebrates have large brains. People are the smartest vertebrates. We can learn many things!

8

Five senses

Vertebrates have **senses**. I have five senses. My senses are **sight**, **hearing**, **smell**, **taste**, and **touch**.

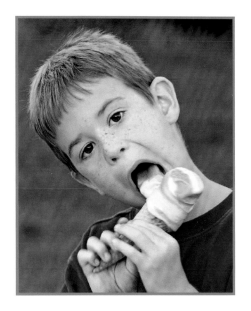

I taste with my tongue.

I see with my eyes.

I hear with my ears.

I touch with my fingers.

I smell with my nose.

9

What do I need?

Air, water, sunshine, soil, and rocks are **non-living things**. These things are not made of cells. Non-living things are very important to me. I could not stay alive without them.

I need water

My body is made mostly of water. I need to drink water all day long to keep my body healthy. I also take baths in water and wash my clothes in water. I love to swim and play in water, too.

I need air

I need to breathe air to survive. I breathe air using my **lungs**. The part of air I **inhale**, or breathe in, is called **oxygen**. The part of air I **exhale**, or breathe out, is called **carbon dioxide**. Plants take in carbon dioxide. Plants release oxygen. They make the air fresh for us to breathe. These girls are planting a tree to make the air fresher to breathe.

I need sunlight

Sunlight keeps me warm. My body needs to be warm to stay alive. Without sunlight, the world would be cold and dark.

Without sunlight, I could not see the beautiful colors of butterflies.

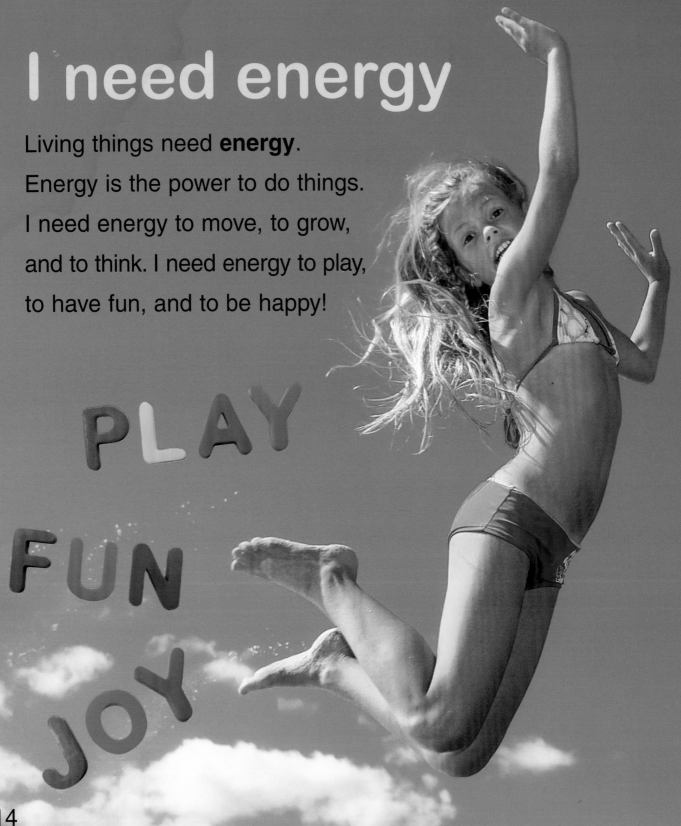

I need energy

Living things need **energy**.
Energy is the power to do things.
I need energy to move, to grow,
and to think. I need energy to play,
to have fun, and to be happy!

PLAY

FUN

JOY

14

All energy comes from the sun. Plants take in the sun's energy through their leaves. Plants use the energy to make food. The energy of the sun is in all these fruits.

I need food!

Plants can get energy from sunshine, but people need to eat food to get energy. The energy of the sun is in plant foods and in foods that come from animals. Most people eat both kinds of food.

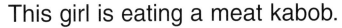

This girl is eating a meat kabob.

Which foods come from plants? Which foods come from animals? Make a list of all the foods shown here that come from plants. Make a list of the foods that come from animals.

I need people

I need other people. I need my family. I need to be part of a **community**. A community is a place where people live. It is also the people who live in that place.

I am part of a family who loves me.
I am part of a school community.

Earth is a big community that
I share with many people!

Some people have
different beliefs.
Some people live
in faraway places.

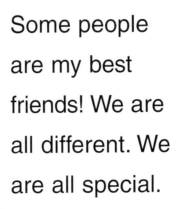

Some people
are my best
friends! We are
all different. We
are all special.

19

I need other things

I need a place where I can feel safe. I feel safe in my home. My home protects me from wind, rain, snow, and the hot sun. My home is a place where I sleep, eat, and have fun. It is a place to which I can invite my friends. I am very lucky to have a home. Not everyone has a home.

I need clothes. My brother and I like to play in the snow. We wear jackets, hats, and boots to keep us warm. We have summer clothes, too.

I need to sing. I love music!

I need to study so I can become a doctor.

I need to be me!

I grow and change

Some animals **hatch** from eggs, but mammals are **born**. I did not hatch from an egg like a bird. I am a mammal, and I was born a baby, just like this one. I could not walk or talk, but I can do both now!

I did not hatch from an egg in a nest. I was born in a hospital.

There is a new baby in my family. Once I was as small as he is. I grew. I learned to walk and talk. I am still growing and changing. I go to school now. I can read and write. When I grow up, I can have babies, too. Growing, changing, and having babies is called a **life cycle**. A new life cycle starts with each baby that is born.

Life cycle

Living things grow and change. They can make babies when they become adults.

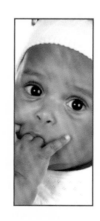

baby

growing child

teenager

adult and baby

Words to know and Index

hatch

animals
pages 4, 5,
8, 16, 17, 22

babies (life cycle)
pages 22-23

cells
pages
6-7, 10

food
pages 5,
15, 16-17

home
page 20

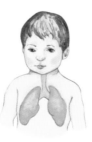

lungs
page 12

people
pages 4, 5, 6,
8, 16, 18-19

plants
pages 4, 5,
12, 15, 16, 17

senses
page 9

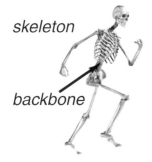
skeleton

backbone

vertebrates
pages 8, 9

water
pages 5, 10, 11

Other index words
air pages 5, 10, 12
brains pages 6, 7, 8
energy pages 14-15, 16
non-living things page 10
sunshine pages 5, 10, 13,
    15, 16, 20